eXplore

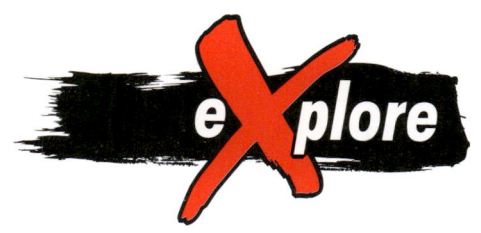

DIVING ON A CORAL REEF

The Wonders of a Coral Reef

R.T. Watts

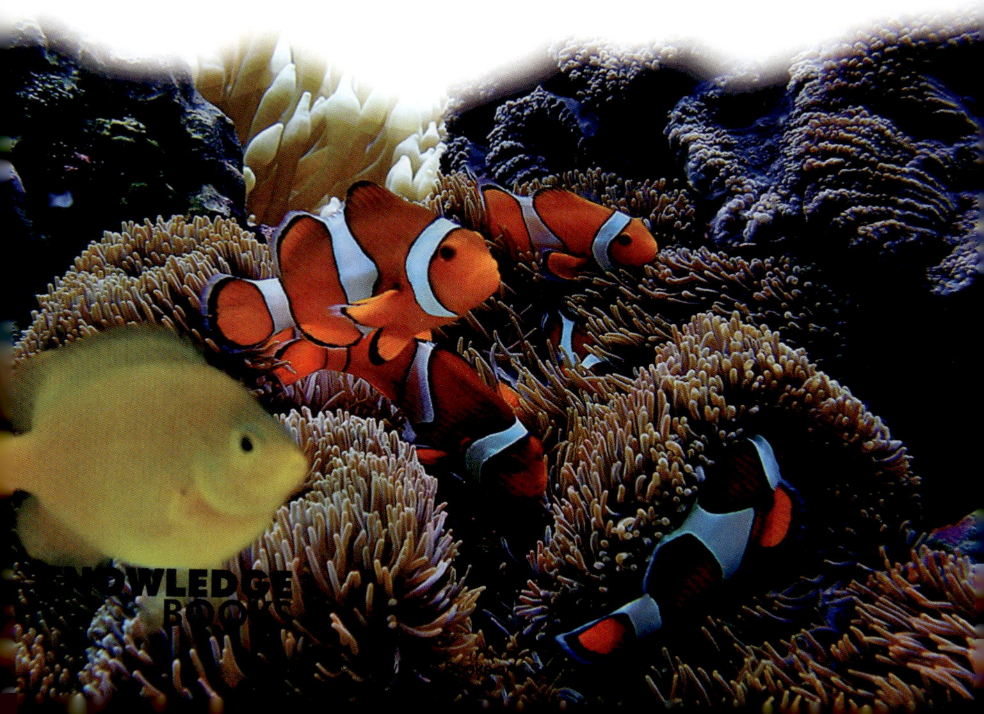

Teacher Notes:

This serves as a general outline of coral reef systems. The recreational opportunities of coral reefs are considered along with the responsibilities. The threats to our reef systems are many and need to be resolved to reverse declines. This chapter book is ideally suited to a conservation-themed science lesson, or a social sciences unit on conservation requirements.

Discussion points for consideration:

1. What is coral? How does a coral reef grow? Describe some forms of coral?

2. Which activities cause reef damage and how can you prevent this?

3. Coral can be damaged by physical means, or chemical means. What are some physical means of reef damage? What are chemical ways of damaging the reef? How can these be stopped and fixed?

Sight words, difficult to decode words, and infrequent words to be introduced and practiced before reading this book:

chemicals, sewerage, coral, Barrier, Mackerel, Barracuda, Trevally, branches, possible, cowrie, Australia, beautiful, possible, explore, animal, different, fantastic, releasing, passenger, different, spawns, temperature, larvae, damaged, together, polluted, bright.

Contents

1. What is Coral?
2. Where are Coral Reefs?
3. Types of Coral
4. Life on a Coral Reef
5. Caring for Coral Reefs
6. Fishing on the Reef

1. What is Coral?

Australia has beautiful coral reefs. It has the world's longest coral reef called the Great Barrier Reef.

What is coral? Coral is a living animal. There are many types of coral. On the Great Barrier Reef, there are over 600 types of coral. Coral comes in all kinds of shapes and colours, including purple, pink, red, blue, green, and yellow. Some coral are soft like rubber and others are hard. Hard coral can look and feel like stone.

How does coral eat? Coral eat small things that move around in the water. The coral waves its arms to move these tiny plants and animals into its mouth.

Small plants called algae live in the coral. Little plants use light to make sugar. The coral takes the sugar from the algae. Corals use this energy to grow and form the hard coral.

Coral grows below the surface of the water. The dead coral can be washed into piles. The dead coral breaks up into small pieces. These coral islands are made of coral sand. These beaches can become land where plants can grow. Turtles and birds may nest on these coral islands.

The coral island has now formed and is protected from the big waves by the coral reef. The Great Barrier Reef has many coral islands.

Some corals glow at night. These corals can glow different colors. Diving on a coral reef at night is great fun. The glow from some corals is fantastic. This image shows coral spawning, which is the releasing of eggs at night.

Coral spawns every year. The water temperature has to be right, and the moon must be just past full. Spawning forms little critters called larvae. The larvae swim across the reef to new areas. When the new larvae find a free spot, they begin to form new coral. This coral may start to build a new reef or repair a broken part of the reef. This is the way the reef grows and fixes damaged parts.

2. Where are Coral Reefs?

Coral reefs are found in warm waters across many oceans. The world's biggest is the Great Barrier Reef in Queensland, Australia.

In the Top End of Australia, corals grow in many places including Western Australia and the Northern Territory.

Corals grow across the world in many seas and oceans. Corals grow across the South Pacific islands, Indonesia, Papua New Guinea and the Philippines. Corals are found in all the oceans of the world. Most of the world's coral reefs are in the Pacific Ocean and the Indian Ocean.

Coral needs the water to be warm but not too warm. If it is too warm, the coral will die.

Coral grows together to form a reef. The reef protects the coral from waves. The waves will break the coral, so the coral forms away from the waves.

Coral reefs have many different animals and plants. Coral supports all sorts of life including many fish, plants, and other animals. Coral reefs form in clear water. If the water is muddy, unclear, cold, or dirty, coral will not grow. Many places close to towns, farms and cities have water which is dirty. These waters cannot grow coral. The water needs to be bright and clean.

If the water is too deep, coral cannot grow. Coral cannot grow without sunlight to feed the algae. If the algae cannot get light, it cannot make energy. The hard corals can only grow in shallow waters where sunlight is strong. The water has to be very clear and clean. Below 160 feet, the water starts to get darker as the light fades.

Coral grows over many thousands of years. It slowly rises to the water surface. The coral forms a platform. This becomes the coral reef. On the outside, the surf breaks on the coral. On the inside, calm waters allow coral to grow. It is in these shallow lagoons that you find a lot of different corals.

Many things need to be right for coral to grow. The reef needs clean and clear water. The temperature of the water has to be warm. The coral cannot grow in deep water as there is not enough light.

Dirty water from rivers or bays can kill coral. The coral cannot live as there is no light in the water. Water coming from farms may poison the coral. This water may contain stuff which was used to kill plants and insects. Water coming from ships may be filthy. Care has to be taken all the time.

3. Types of Coral

There are many types of coral on a reef. On the Great Barrier Reef, there are over 600 types.

Corals are named by their shape and color. It is hard to know the exact name of a coral. We will just use their form and color to name the corals. These are some of the corals you will see on the Great Barrier Reef.

Staghorn Coral is a common coral and forms large branches. Small fish hide from big fish in coral.

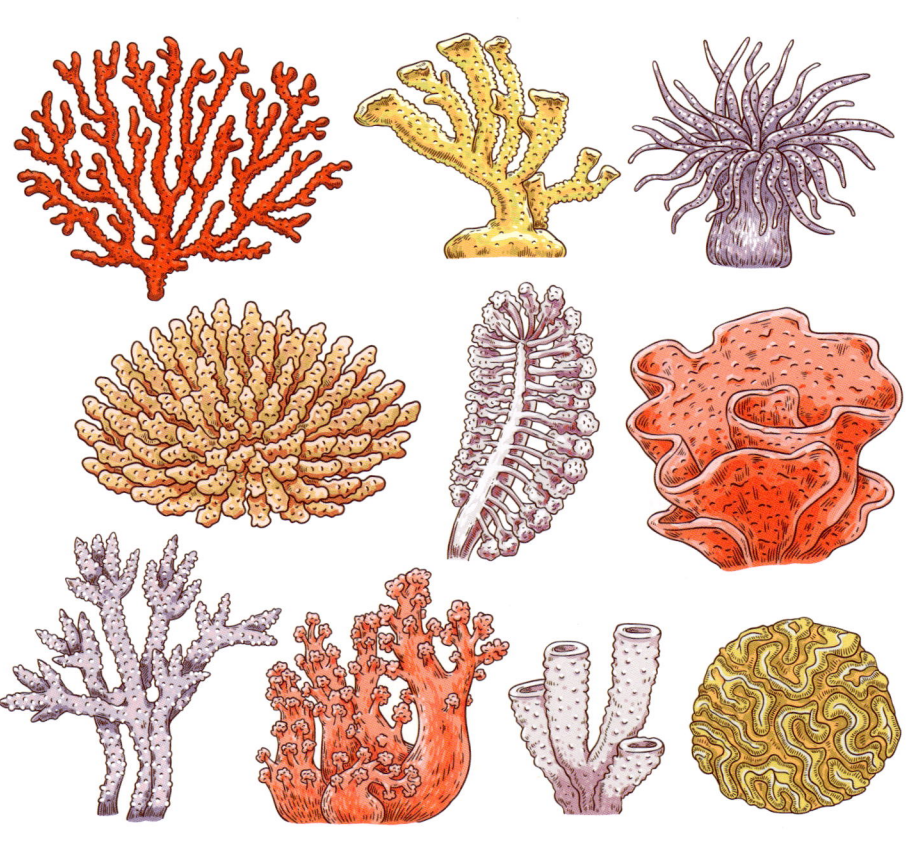

Brain Coral is a giant ball shape. It can be different colors from yellow to pink. Some fish feed on the smooth surface of the coral. They eat the coral which contains the algae. Brain Coral can be the size of a school desk.

Fan Coral is a fine coral which is shaped like a thin tree. It forms a giant fan and is stuck to the coral by a strong cement. It has its fan moving to catch food from the water flow. It does this by filter feeding. These are beautiful corals which can grow as big as a person.

Corals grow up like a tree, or grow out like a mushroom. Strong waves will break some forms of coral. The corals with flat round shapes are not broken by waves.

The coral on a reef does not stay the same. It is always in a battle with the other corals. Corals try to grow as much as possible. Some corals grow faster than other corals. The coral reef will look different in certain areas. In the very shallow parts of the coral reef, round, flat corals grow better as they are not dry for a long time at low tide. The big coral prefer deeper water otherwise they will dry out at low tide.

There are many animals which need coral to survive. Sea slugs can be found on the coral reefs. Sea slugs eat the algae out of the coral sand. The sea slug keeps the coral reef clean and bright. If all the sea slugs are taken as food, the coral reef sand starts to go green.

4. Life on a Coral Reef

The coral reef may have coral sand forming an island. The island may have a little forest of trees. The forest may allow sea birds to nest. On the Great Barrier Reef, there are many islands where birds can make nests. These nests allow the sea birds to lay eggs and hatch chicks.

The sand on the island can be used by turtles to lay eggs. The turtles cover the eggs with sand. The warm sand hatches the turtle eggs. There are many islands on the reef which turtles use to hatch their eggs. To see the little turtles hatch is very special and happens every year.

Shells cover the coral beaches. Together these shells and the coral make up the beach. The shells break into smaller and smaller pieces until they are just like sand.

Shells are the remains of animals that live on, and near, the reef. The shell itself is the house to hold the animal. These are called shellfish or molluscs. A garden snail is also a mollusc.

The shells are beautiful shapes and colors. Molluscs feed on small algae and keep the reef clean.

Cowries are reef shells. The living shells are very important for the coral reef and should not be touched. The empty shell that is washed on to the beach no longer contains animals. Hermit crabs and other little critters still hide in the empty shells, so they are still important to the reef animals.

Long ago, cowrie shells were used as money in some countries. Cowrie shells were used as money in Asia and Africa. The Chinese symbol for money is still the shape of a cowrie shell; 貝

5. Caring for Coral Reefs

Coral can die if things change. Some reefs die and never return. Coral reefs can be wiped out by a storm or by humans.

Australia has the Great Barrier Reef, which is the biggest coral reef in the world. People come from all over the world to see this beautiful wonder.

Farms along the coast grow a lot of our food. Farms grow sugar cane, bananas, tomatoes, pineapples, pumpkins, mangoes, nuts, and lots more. Farmers work very hard to make a living. Pests eat and destroy the plants.

Farmers need to use chemicals. Without the chemicals, the crops get eaten, will not grow, or die. Corals are killed by these chemicals. These chemicals must not get into the creeks or rivers. Farmers are building ponds, mangrove forests, and little swamps to catch and hold the farm's run-off water. It also helps hold muddy water, which would block the light and kill the coral. It is like Nature's sewer plant. The water is cleaned and then goes into the creeks or rivers. The rivers take the water out to the coral reefs. If the water contains chemicals or mud, then the coral will die.

Farmers and scientists are working to stop this chemical damage of the reef. We need to have both food and the reef!

We need to protect all areas of the reef. Each time coral is broken, it means people in the future can not see this beautiful coral. If a coral reef gets anchor damage by a lot of boats, then coral does not have time to grow back. The coral dies, the fish go away, and the beautiful coral is gone. Boats need to be very careful where they anchor to stop damage to the coral.

Boats need to make sure they do not release chemicals. Some boats have spilt fuel, sewerage, and chemicals into the water. These liquids will kill the coral.

Australia has Green Zones on the Reef. These are special protection areas where you cannot fish or stay.

People love our reef! More and more people visit the Great Barrier Reef every year. It is our reef, and we are looking after this for everyone in the world. When you visit the reef, make sure you help make it better.

Boats travel through the reef. There are sailing boats, fishing boats, container ships, ore ships, passenger ships, and many others. These boats can damage the reef.

Sailing and fishing boats love to visit the reef. Some boats throw their anchors on to the coral. This holds the anchor tight and stops the boat moving. Anchors smash the coral. The broken coral will take many years to grow back.

Fishing is a lot of fun. The reef has many types of fish. People go on their holidays to fish on the Great Barrier Reef. As long as you are not greedy, you do not damage the fish numbers. Fish grow, get eaten by other fish, and die! The fish that you take will be replaced by another fish that will grow. But do not be greedy! Do not catch more than you can eat.

If too many fish are taken, some may not be replaced. This will cause fish numbers to drop and disappear. It will be sad to see beautiful fish go from the reef.

You have a limit on the number of fish caught. This is called your 'bag limit'. This is the law, and you will be fined if you are over the limit.

Coral bleaching happens when the water is too warm and the algae and the coral dies.

If the water is too warm, the coral starts to die. The warm water can be caused by the poor movement of water, bright light, or very hot weather.

The changing climate is having an effect on the coral. Coral is dying in parts of the Indian Ocean and the Pacific, including the Great Barrier Reef.

It is easy to see this dead coral as it is white. This is called 'coral bleaching'.

The Crown of Thorns Starfish is a threat to coral. It overeats the coral and wrecks the reef. Other animals like the Parrotfish also eat coral. The problem is that the starfish is getting out of control and eating everything on the platform.

This starfish is eaten by fish and other animals on the reef. Most of the time, the starfish numbers are not too high. However, polluted water can also kill the fish that feed on the starfish.

The Great Barrier Reef is too big for the Crown of Thorns Starfish to be completely removed. This would take many divers a long time to complete.

Coral reefs can be polluted by garbage. Ships and boats throwing rubbish and sewerage into the ocean may damage the reef. This can cause some fish and coral larvae to die. This changes the types of corals, plants, and animals on the reef.

The reef is now out of balance from its natural state. Once it changes, one type of coral, animal, or plant can take over. This includes lots of Crown of Thorns Starfish, too many Staghorn Coral, or green algae growing over the coral.

6. Fishing on the Reef

A huge variety of fish live on and near the reef. These coral reefs are famous for fishing. Big fish can be caught. Some of the fish live hiding in the coral. Other fish live on the outside of the reef. There are over 1500 types of fish on the reef. Sharks are very common, with over 134 different sharks on the Great Barrier Reef.

Fishing on a coral reef is great fun. If you are fishing from a boat over coral, you can catch all sorts of fish. One of the favorite fish to catch is the Coral Trout. It is a sneaky fish which hides under the coral and looks above for things to eat.

Fishing on a coral reef can be tricky, and you need to know what the fish will do when it is caught. You need to be careful when catching this fish as it will run under the coral. Your fishing line will tangle, and you will lose your hooks, sinkers, line, and bait. It is important to be careful and make sure that your line is not tangled on the reef. Dolphins, turtles, and other sea animals can get caught in the tangle and die. The fishing line takes a long time to break down in the saltwater. The broken fishing line will be on the coral reef for a very long time. Do not leave ropes, fishing lines, or anchors in the water.

If you fish just off the reef, you find the big fish. These big fish eat the reef fish. They have razor-sharp teeth and their body is shaped like a bullet. These are the fastest fish in the water. The big, fast fish travel close to the surface. Below the fast predator fish are the sharks. They eat anything that comes too close.

The predator fish cruise around the reef looking for other fish to eat. The other fish quickly dart amongst the coral when they see them. Spanish Mackerel, Barracuda, reef sharks, Bluefish, and Giant Trevally are some of the fighting fish people like catching. The Spanish Mackerel is a favorite as it is a great fighting fish and good to eat. Reef fishing is a favourite hobby for many people.

Word Bank

algae
chemicals
sewerage
coral
Barrier
Mackerel
Barracuda
Trevally
branches
possible
cowrie
Australia
beautiful
possible

cowrie
explore
animal
different
fantastic
releasing
passenger
different
spawns
temperature
larvae
damaged